Rise from the Shadows:
A Journey to Freedom

by

Emma Grace Taylor

Emma Grace Taylor

Epilogue

This book is dedicated to all the women who have endured and survived domestic violence. May your healing journey be filled with strength, hope, and the unwavering belief that you are worthy of love and happiness. May you find the courage to break free, the support to rebuild, and the love you deserve.

Rise from the Shadows: A Journey of Freedom

Table of Contents

Chapter 1
Shadows of My Past

The sound of breaking glass shattered the silence of the night, jolting me awake. My heart pounded as I threw off the covers and crept out of bed, my tiny feet making no sound on the wooden floor. The house was dark, the only light coming from the kitchen where shadows danced on the walls. As I reached the top of the stairs, I could see the source of the commotion: my father, towering over my mother, his face twisted in rage.

"Don't you dare talk back to me!" he bellowed, his voice thick with alcohol. My mother was on the floor, clutching her cheek where he had struck her. Her eyes, wide with fear, met mine for a fleeting moment before she looked away, ashamed.

I froze, my small body trembling with fear. I wanted to run, to hide, but my feet were rooted to the spot. My father's eyes, wild with fury, shifted towards me. "What the fuck are you looking at?" he bellowed, staggering towards me. His hand came up again, and I braced myself for the blow. When it landed, pain exploded in my head, and I crumpled to the floor beside my mother.

The days that followed were a blur of pain and confusion. My mother, with her bruised face and broken spirit, tried to comfort me, but there was little solace to be found. The house, once a place of warmth and safety, had become a prison filled with fear and dread. I learned to navigate the landmines of my father's anger, always careful not to provoke him. But no matter how hard I tried, it never seemed to be enough.

The abuse was not limited to physical violence. My father's words were weapons, slicing through my self-esteem and leaving deep, invisible wounds. "You're worthless, you know that?" he would say, his voice dripping with contempt. "No one will ever love you. You're just like your mother." These words echoed in my mind, shaping my perception of myself and the world around me.

I remember one ruthless night when my father came home drunker than usual. The stench of alcohol clung to him as he stumbled through the door, his eyes glazed with anger. My mother tried calming him down, but it only worsened things. He grabbed her by the hair, dragging her across the room as she screamed in pain.

Terrified, I hid under the kitchen table, my small body trembling with fear. I watched in horror as my father struck my mother again and again, his fury unrelenting. I wanted to help her, to make him stop, but I was paralyzed with fear. I felt so helpless, so powerless.

After what felt like an eternity, my father finally stormed out of the house, leaving my mother crumpled on the floor. I crawled out from under the table and rushed to her side, my heart breaking at the sight of her bruised and battered face. She looked at me with tear-filled eyes and whispered, "It's okay, Emma. Mommy's fine. Daddy has the devil in him right now."

But I knew she wasn't okay. None of us were.

The nights on the weekend were the hardest. I lay in bed, wide awake, straining to hear any sound that might indicate another outburst. Every creak of the floorboards, every rustle of the wind outside, set my heart racing. I slept with a small flashlight under my pillow, ready to escape quickly. The dark corners of my room became places where my imagination conjured up the worst scenarios, each more terrifying than the last.

At school, I put on a brave face, smiling and laughing with my friends, but inside I was crumbling. The fear and shame were like a constant weight on my shoulders, dragging me down. I became withdrawn, avoiding eye contact and avoiding any situation that might draw attention to myself. I was afraid that anyone would see the truth if they looked too closely.

My mother, a teacher's aide, tried to protect me as best she could, but there was only so much she could do. She was trapped in the same nightmare, struggling to survive each day. I often wondered why she didn't leave, why she stayed with a man who caused us so much pain. But as I grew older, I began to understand. Leaving was more complex than walking out the door. It required resources, support, and the belief that life *could* be better.

Despite the darkness that overshadowed our lives, there were moments of light. My mother's love was a beacon of hope, a reminder that not everything was terrible. She would hold me close, whispering words of comfort and encouragement. "You're strong, my sweet girl," she would say. "One day, you'll rise above all of this."

Those words became my mantra, a lifeline I clung to in the darkest moments. I promised myself that I would escape the cycle of violence and build a better life for myself. But the journey ahead was long and fraught with challenges, and the road to freedom was anything but easy.

The scars of my past ran deep, but they also shaped me into the person I would become. They taught me resilience, strength, and the importance of self-worth. As I moved forward, I carried the lessons of my childhood, determined to break the chains that had bound me for so long.

Each day, I found small ways to cope. I immersed myself in books, escaping into worlds where the heroes always triumphed, and justice was served. I wrote in my journal, pouring my fears and dreams onto the pages. I found solace in music, letting the melodies wash over me and soothe my troubled heart.

As I grew older, I began to dream of a future beyond the walls of my home. I imagined going to college, starting a career, and building a life free from violence and fear. These dreams gave me hope and strength, even on the darkest days. They reminded me that there was a world beyond my father's anger where I could find peace and happiness.

The journey was long and complex, but with each step forward, I grew stronger. I learned to stand up for myself, to set boundaries, and to believe in my worth. Along the way, I found allies, people who supported me and believed in me. Slowly but surely, I began to build the life I had always dreamed of.

Chapter 2
Patterns in Pain

The cycle of abuse didn't end with my father. It followed me like a shadow, a dark cloud I couldn't escape. As I grew older, I found myself drawn to men who echoed his violence. My first boyfriend, James, seemed charming initially, with his easy smile and smooth words. He made me feel special as if I were the only person who mattered. But it wasn't long before his sweet compliments turned into cutting insults.

"You're so fucking stupid," he would say, rolling his eyes at me. "No wonder no one else wants you. Even your father didn't want you." Each insult chipped away at my self-esteem until I believed his words. I thought I was lucky to have him, that no one else would ever love me.

James's insults soon turned into physical abuse. He would grab my arm tightly, leaving bruises, or shove me against the wall during arguments. I tried to excuse his behavior, telling myself that he was just stressed or that I had somehow provoked him. The fear and shame kept me silent, convinced that I somehow deserved the pain.

My job as an Administrative Assistant was my sanctuary. I could escape the turmoil of this "love" life in this place. I worked for a handsome man in his early thirties, a kind and respectful boss who treated me with the dignity I had long forgotten I deserved. He appreciated my work, often complimenting me on my efficiency and dedication. But his kindness became a source of suspicion for James.

James was constantly accusing me of sleeping with my boss. His jealousy was relentless, and no reassurance could convince him otherwise. The situation escalated in

April, on Administrative Professional's Day. My boss surprised me with pink roses and took me to lunch to show appreciation for my hard work. I was touched by his gesture, feeling valued and recognized.

Seeing the roses in my handset, James was off when I returned home that evening. "Who gave you those?" he demanded, his eyes narrowing with anger. "My boss," I replied, trying to keep my voice steady. It's Administrative Professional's Day."

James's face twisted with rage. "I knew it! I knew you were sleeping with him!" He grabbed the roses from my hand and threw them across the room. I tried to explain, to make him understand that it was just a kind gesture, but he wasn't listening. His accusations grew louder and more vicious, and I felt my heart sink as I realized there was nothing I could say to change his mind.

The next few weeks were a nightmare. James's jealousy reached new heights, and he monitored my every move. He would call me multiple times at work, demanding to know where I was and who I was with. The constant suspicion was exhausting, and I felt like I was walking on eggshells, trying to avoid anything that might set him off.

Christmas came, and I bought James a special gift—a bottle of his favorite cologne. I hoped it would show him how much I cared and wanted to make things work between us. When he opened the gift, I saw a flicker of surprise in his eyes, but it quickly turned to something darker.

"Why did you buy me this?" he asked, his voice low and dangerous. "I thought you'd like it," I replied, my heart pounding. "It's your favorite."

His eyes narrowed. "Did you buy your boss something too?" The question took me by surprise, and before I could respond, his fist came crashing down on my face. The pain was immediate and excruciating. I fell to the floor, clutching my face, as tears streamed down my cheeks.

James stood over me, his face contorted with rage. "You're a whore," he spat. "You don't deserve anything." He stormed out of the room, leaving me crumpled on the floor, my face throbbing with pain.

The following day, I looked in the mirror and barely recognized myself. My eye was swollen shut, the skin around it dark and bruised. I tried to cover it with makeup, but it was no use. I couldn't see out of my eye for two weeks. When my coworkers asked me what happened, I lied and told them I hit myself in the face. I was too embarrassed to tell them the truth, too ashamed to admit that I was in an abusive relationship.

The fear and shame kept me isolated. I couldn't bear to tell anyone what was happening, convinced they would judge or blame me for staying. I felt utterly alone, drowning in a sea of despair.

James's jealousy and rage became a constant presence in my life. I never knew what might set him off, what innocent action might be twisted into a betrayal. The most minor things—a smile, a friendly conversation, a kind gesture—could spark his fury. I lived in a constant state of anxiety, always on edge, always afraid.

Despite the abuse, there were moments when I saw a glimmer of the man I had fallen in love with. James could be charming and affectionate; sometimes, he made me feel truly loved. These moments were rare, but they kept me hoping that things might change and that the man I loved might come back to me.

But the abuse continued, and the hope that things might get better began to fade. I felt trapped in a never-ending cycle of violence and fear, unable to see a way out. The shame of my situation kept me silent, convinced that I somehow deserved the pain.

It wasn't until much later that I realized the truth: the abuse was not my fault. I didn't deserve to be treated this way. No one does. It was this realization that gave me the strength to start thinking about leaving, to begin imagining a life free from fear and pain.

The journey ahead was long and fraught with challenges, but I knew I had to take it for myself and the hope of a better future.

Chapter 3
Ray Allen: The Final Straw

In my twenties, I met Ray Allen. He was a mail carrier and initially seemed different from the others. He was attentive, constantly checking in to ensure I was okay. He listened to me and made me laugh, and for a while, I thought I had finally found someone to treat me with the kindness and respect I had always longed for. But it didn't take long for his true colors to show.

Ray was cheap and stingy with his money in a way that went beyond frugality. Every dinner with his family, every gift for birthdays or holidays, every get-together—I paid for it all. He never spent a dime. When we went out to eat, he would buy me kids' meals at Chick-fil-A or McDonald's, saying it was what I deserved. If I wanted a fancy dinner, I had to buy it myself.

We both collected Snoopy items, a shared interest that initially brought us closer. At the local mall, there was a contest to win a vast Snoopy stuffed doll. I entered and won, thrilled at the prospect of adding it to my collection. But Ray took it home, claiming it as his own. It was a small yet significant reminder of how little he valued me.

One evening, he decided to grill burgers. As he handed me mine, it was burnt to a crisp. He looked at me with disdain and said, "You don't deserve a better burger because you're just worth it." He then gave his dog a perfectly cooked burger. The humiliation and heartbreak were unbearable, but still, like an idiot, I stayed.

When my mother died, Ray Allen's cruelty reached new heights. As I mourned her loss, he sneered, "I am glad your mother died; now you have more time to spend with me." His words cut through me like a knife, the pain almost too much to bear. But I stayed, convinced that I deserved no better.

As our relationship progressed, the emotional abuse intensified. Ray's controlling nature became more evident. He manipulated me, twisted my words, and made me doubt my sanity. He isolated me from my friends and family, convincing me that they didn't care about me and that I was better off with him. The constant emotional turmoil took a toll on my mental health, and I felt like I was losing myself.

When we finally broke up, Ray didn't just let me go. He followed me everywhere. One night, during a girls' night out, my best friend Christy noticed a familiar car trailing us. "Isn't that Ray's car?" she asked, her voice tinged with concern. I felt a chill run down my spine. But Christy was brilliant. She drove straight to the police station. Ray sped off as soon as he realized he had been tricked.

Desperate to move on, I started posting Romance Ads, thinking it might be a better way to meet new people. But Ray found a way to infiltrate my life once again. He broke into my voicemail and called the men I was getting to know, spreading vile lies about me. He told them I was a thief and that I was HIV positive. One man called me, deeply concerned, to tell me about Ray's accusations.

This was the breaking point. I finally gathered the nerve to contact Ray's parents. When I called, his father answered. I tried to explain the situation to make him understand that I needed Ray to leave me alone. His response was curt and dismissive: "Not at this time," and then he hung up the phone.

About a year later, my sister threw me a surprise birthday party. I hadn't told her about my problems with Ray, hoping to keep the event light-hearted and joyous. I was shocked that Ray showed up, begging me to return to him. I was dating someone else then—Andre—a good man who treated me respectfully and kindly. I told Ray, "No," standing firm despite the fear in my stomach.

Ray's face twisted in anger. As he walked out of the house, he spat, "I hope you die soon, you stupid bitch." Those were the last words he said to me and the last time I saw him.

But the damage had been done. The constant fear, the relentless harassment—it wore me down. I broke it off with Andre, convinced that my life would never get better, that Ray's shadow would always loom over me. The pain was overwhelming. I hated myself. I wanted to die.

Ray had taken everything from me—my self-esteem, sense of safety, and hope for the future. I felt like a shell of my former self, lost in a whirlwind of pain and hate. But even in the darkest moments, a tiny spark of resilience remained. I knew I had to find a way out to reclaim my life and dignity.

The journey ahead was long and fraught with challenges, but I knew I had to take it for myself and the hope of a better future.

Chapter 4
Breaking Free

reaking it off with Andre was the hardest thing I had ever done. I cared about him, but I was terrified of the unknown and falling in love all over again. I was unsure that I would be condemning myself to a lifetime of misery and abuse. So, I packed my bags, took a deep breath, walked out the door, and grabbed a bus to Monterrey, Mexico—where I knew Ray would never go.

The first few weeks were the most challenging. I had no money, no job, and nowhere to go. I stayed with friends, slept on a park bench when I couldn't and tried to piece my life together. The fear of Ray finding me was constant, but the hope of a better future kept me going.

I sought therapy, joined support groups, learned self-defense, and slowly began to rebuild my sense of self-worth. Each step forward was a victory, no matter how small. I realized that I was not alone; many women and men had faced similar battles and emerged stronger.

Therapy was a lifeline, helping me to process the trauma and begin to heal. My therapist helped me to see that the abuse was not my fault and that I deserved love and respect. She taught me coping strategies, helped me to set boundaries, and supported me as I navigated the difficult journey of healing.

One of the most profound moments in therapy was when I realized the patterns of abuse in my life. I began to understand how my father's violence had shaped my relationships and how I had been conditioned to accept mistreatment as usual. This realization was painful, but it was also empowering. It meant I could change that I could break the cycle.

The support groups were equally invaluable. Hearing the stories of other survivors was both heartbreaking and empowering. These women had faced unimaginable pain and hardship, yet they had found the strength to survive and rebuild their lives. Their courage and resilience inspired me, and their friendship and support gave me the strength to keep going.

I also began to reconnect with my family and friends. It wasn't easy initially, as I had pushed them away for so long, but their love and support were unwavering. They helped me to find a job, a place to live, and a sense of stability. With their help, I began to rebuild my life, one step at a time.

One of the most supportive figures in my journey was Veronica—a new friend and sister I made when I arrived in Monterrey.

She has always been there for me, even when I was too afraid to let her in. She helped me find a place to live, drove me to therapy sessions, and constantly encouraged me. With her help, I began to see that I deserved better and was worthy of love and respect.

As I started rebuilding my life, I also began to rediscover my passions. I threw myself into my work, finding joy and fulfillment in my career. I reconnected with my love for writing, pouring my experiences and emotions onto my journal pages. These activities were therapeutic, helping me process my trauma and find a sense of purpose.

The journey was not without setbacks. There were days when the weight of my past felt too heavy to bear when the memories of Ray's abuse would overwhelm me. But each time I stumbled, I got back up. Each small victory— a completed therapy session, a supportive conversation with a friend, a moment of peace—was a testament to my resilience and strength.

Chapter 5
Love and Understanding

Years later, I met Damian. He was kind, patient, and understanding. Our relationship was not without its challenges, but the difference was profound. There was no violence, only love and mutual respect. We have been together for twelve years, building a life filled with laughter and support.

Damian and I have fights and disagreements like any couple, but they are resolved with words, not fists. He has shown me what true love looks like, teaching me that I am worthy of respect and kindness. I have found a sense of peace and security that I never thought possible with him.

Our relationship has not been without its struggles. My past trauma has made it difficult for me to trust, and there have been times when I have pushed Damian away out of fear. But he has always been patient and understanding, giving me the space and support I need to heal.

Damian has taught me that it is possible to have disagreements without violence. We have learned to communicate openly and honestly, to listen to each other, and to work through our problems together. Our relationship is built on mutual respect and love, and it has made all the difference.

One of the most significant moments in our relationship was when I finally told Damian about my past. I had been afraid to share my story, worried that he would see me differently or that the memories would become too painful. But Damian listened with compassion and understanding. He held me as I cried, reassuring me that my past did not define me and that he loved me for who I was.

With Damian's support, I continued to work on my healing. I still attended therapy, practiced self-care, and leaned on my support network. The journey was not easy, but it was worth it. I found a sense of peace and happiness I never thought possible, and I was grateful daily for the love and support that helped me get here.

Our relationship has also taught me the importance of boundaries and self-respect. I learned to assert my needs and to communicate openly about my feelings. Damian respected my boundaries and encouraged me to prioritize my well-being. This mutual respect and understanding have been the foundation of our relationship, allowing us to grow together and support each other through life's challenges.

Over the years, Damian and I have built a life filled with love, laughter, and adventure. We have traveled together, explored new hobbies, and created countless memories. Each moment of joy has reminded me of how far I have come and of the love and happiness I deserve.

Chapter 6
A Message to My Sisters

To every woman (or man) reading this who feels trapped in a cycle of abuse knows that there *is* a way out. You are *not* alone. Reach out for help, believe in your worth, and take that courageous step towards freedom. Life beyond the shadows is possible; you deserve to live it fully.

I know that it can feel impossible to leave and that the fear and shame can be overwhelming. But I also know that there is hope. Some people care about you, want to help you, and believe in your worth. Reach out to them, lean on them, and let them support you.

Leaving an abusive relationship is not easy, and it will not happen overnight. It will take time, effort, and a lot of courage. But it is possible. Take it one step at a time, and remember you are not alone. A whole community of survivors has faced the same struggles and emerged stronger.

Believe in yourself, and know that you deserve love and respect. You are worthy of happiness and have the strength to create a better future for yourself. Take that first step, and don't look back.

Find solace in the small victories, the moments of peace and joy that remind you of your worth. Surround yourself with people who uplift and support you. Seek out therapy and support groups, and allow yourself the time and space to heal.

Remember, your past does not define you. You have the power to create a new story, one filled with love, respect, and happiness. It will be a journey, but it is a journey worth taking.

National Hotlines and Resources

National Domestic Violence Hotline (US):
Phone: 1-800-799-SAFE (7233)
TTY: 1-800-787-3224
Text "START" to 88788
Website: www.thehotline.org

Services: 24/7 confidential support, crisis intervention, safety planning, and resources for victims of domestic violence.

National Coalition Against Domestic Violence (NCADV):
Website: www.ncadv.org

Services: Advocacy, education, and support for victims of domestic violence.

RAINN (Rape, Abuse & Incest National Network):
Phone: 1-800-656-HOPE (4673)
Website: www.rainn.org

Services: Confidential support for sexual assault victims, including crisis intervention and resources. Live Chat is available.

Loveisrespect:
Phone: 1-866-331-9474
TTY: 1-866-331-8453
Text: "LOVEIS" to 22522
Website: www.loveisrespect.org

Services: Support and resources for young people in abusive relationships, including chat and text services.

International Hotlines and Resources

Women's Aid (UK):
Phone: 0808 2000 247 (24-hour helpline)
Website: www.womensaid.org.uk

Services: Support, advocacy, and resources for women and children experiencing domestic violence. Live Chat is available.

Canadian Women's Foundation:
Website: www.canadianwomen.org
Phone: (866) 293-4483

Services: Programs and resources to support women escaping violence, including emergency shelters and legal advice.

Domestic Violence Resource Centre Victoria (Australia):
Phone: (03) 8346 58200
Website: www.dvrcv.org.au

Services: Support, information, and resources for women experiencing domestic violence.

Additional Resources

Local Shelters and Support Services:

Many communities have local shelters, hotlines, and support services specifically for victims of domestic violence. These can often be found through local directories or by contacting national hotlines for referrals.

Legal Assistance:
WomensLaw.org: www.womenslaw.org

Provides legal information and support for victims of domestic violence.

Counseling and Support Groups:

Many organizations offer counseling services and support groups for victims of domestic violence. Contacting national hotlines or local shelters can help connect individuals with these resources.

Tips for Safely Seeking Help

Use Safe Devices: Whenever possible, use a phone or computer that the abuser cannot access to avoid detection.

Document Abuse: Keep a record of incidents, including dates, times, and descriptions of the abuse. This can be important for legal action.

Create a Safety Plan: Plan and prepare for the possibility of leaving an abusive situation. This can include packing an emergency bag, saving money, and identifying a safe place to go.

These resources provide essential support and information for women suffering from domestic abuse, helping them to find safety and rebuild their lives.

Tips for Safely Seeking Help

www.ingramcontent.com/pod-product-compliance
Lightning Source LLC
Chambersburg PA
CBHW050622160726
48003CB00003B/1292